June, 2000

We love you!
For
alice
from
Grandma & Grandpa B.

June 2000

For My Granddaughter

By Lois L. Kaufman

Illustrated by Karen Anagnost

PETER PAUPER PRESS, INC.
WHITE PLAINS, NEW YORK

For Sarah, my darling granddaughter

Illustrations copyright © 1999
Karen Anagnost

Designed by Arlene Greco

Text copyright © 1999
Peter Pauper Press, Inc.
202 Mamaroneck Avenue
White Plains, NY 10601
ISBN 0-88088-387-1
Printed in China
7 6 5 4 3 2

For My
Granddaughter

Tell your
Grandma anything—
she'll understand.

*I*f you had everything
in the world you wanted,
you wouldn't have
enough room to keep it.

When you love
someone, your greatest
pleasure is that
person's happiness.

Some of the friends
you make in your early
years may be your friends
forever. Treasure them.

Take one day at
a time. Remember that
tomorrow is another day
and yesterday is gone,
not to be repeated.

Show affection

generously. It will be

returned, and you'll see

how wonderful it is to be

on the receiving end!

*K*eep busy and
you'll keep happy.

*S*tand up for
what you believe.

$\mathcal{L}$aughter is good

for the body

and the soul.

*L*isten to the sounds
of nature, and serenity and
joy will follow.

*H*appiness means

having something

to hope for.

Be generous;
when you share your good
things you'll enjoy them
even more.

$\mathcal{I}$f you get everything
you want *now*,
you'll have nothing
to look forward to.

*H*appiness is

a highway,

not a destination.

*E*ducation will take you

further than charm.

The way you
behave in public
tells others who you are
and what you are like.

*L*isten to what

other people say,

but decide for yourself.

Take advantage
of modern technology.
It can give you the tools
for a better future.

Keep an open mind.
You never know what will
be helpful to you.

*Y*ou can't please
everybody. Try to please
yourself first
and foremost.

*E*very experience

can teach you something,

if you let it.

⟨෮⟩

$\mathcal{I}$f you take
responsibility for what
you do, you're bound to do
everything to the best of
your ability.

$\mathcal{F}$aultfinding is

never constructive.

Try to be helpful, instead.

*R*emember that you
can't always do everything
by yourself. Don't be
ashamed to ask for help
when you need it.

Acting cheerful

can often make you

feel cheerful.

*M*oney you earn
yourself will be more
satisfying to you
than money that is
given to you.

*G*ive praise generously

when it's deserved.

*S*hare *yourself* and you'll

receive joy in return.

*H*appiness comes from
enjoying what you have,
and from not wanting what
you can't have.

$\mathcal{L}$et your parents
know how much you
appreciate what they've
done for you.

Before you
say something in
anger that you will
regret later, *think!*

Don't be angry at rules
that your parents make.
They're for your own good.

$\mathscr{D}$on't let fear
of failure keep you from
trying something new.

*B*e independent.
Try to judge things
for yourself.

*G*et as much education
as you can. Knowledge
and information are
your best friends.

ᕲ

$\mathcal{B}$e your own person.
Don't let pressure from
others influence you to
do something you know
you shouldn't.

It's easier to form
a good habit than to
get rid of a bad one.

You can look
through your tears
and see a rainbow.

$\mathcal{W}$hen you're
with someone you love,
it isn't always necessary
to talk. Just being together
can be enough.

*M*ake music and
art and nature a constant
part of your life.
All will bring you joy.

$\mathcal{B}$e charitable,

but not boastful about it.

$\mathcal{D}$on't be wasteful.

It's bad for the world.

$\mathcal{T}$rust your instincts.

Feminine intuition

is not a myth.

$\mathcal{W}$hen something
hurtful is on the tip
of your tongue, bite it!

"If at first you don't
succeed, try, try again,"
may be a cliché, but that
doesn't make it any less
valuable as a guide.

$\mathcal{I}$f you have faith

in other people,

it will usually

be justified.

$\mathcal{L}$earn how

to forgive. Sometimes,

be the first to apologize.

$\mathcal{L}$et your

imagination loose.

Creativity will follow.

Be flexible,

but don't bend

your standards.

$\mathcal{W}$orry is

a useless occupation.

Understanding can

chase fear away.

$\mathcal{W}$hen you

make the best of

something, sometimes it

becomes the best.

*E*very day,

try to do one thing

you don't like to do.

*L*ittle acts
of kindness help
you as much as
the recipient.

A walk in the
rain can wash
away the cobwebs
in your mind.

$\mathcal{B}$e tolerant.

Then try to *understand*

what you're tolerating.

A bouquet of weeds

given with love

can be more welcome

than a florist's

best arrangement.

$\mathscr{A}$ccept change.
You're bound
to change, too.

*A*lways try to be just.
If it's within your
power to right an injustice,
go ahead and do it.

$\mathscr{I}$f you make a promise,

be sure to keep it.

$\mathcal{L}$ife has its ups and its

downs. Go with the flow.

*T*ake care of your health.

You want it to last

as long as *you* do!

*B*e careful what you
wish for, because you
might just get it!

$\mathcal{W}$rite "thank you"

notes immediately.

Otherwise you might forget

to write them at all.

$\mathcal{D}$on't accept
limits others set for you.
Let yourself fly.

A friend who loves
you in spite of your
imperfections is a
friend to cherish.

Set aside time to play.

*T*ell your parents

how much you love them.

They love to hear it.

*O*ccasionally,

do something *before* your

mother asks you to do it.

The best is yet to come,
and you can make
it happen.

$\mathcal{B}$e as proud of yourself

as I am of you.